Editors: Tim Inman
        Jan Poppe
        Carlos Ramet

Designer: Adam Baudoux

Photographers: Adam Baudoux
              James Fry
              Tim Inman
              Matt Shaw
              Jonathan Zelanak

Published by: Saginaw Valley State University
              University Center, Michigan 48710

Printed in Midland, Michigan by: McKay Press

ISBN-13: 978-0-61-540574-2

SAGINAW VALLEY
STATE UNIVERSITY

A Seasonal Portrait

Foreword

What makes a destination, an event or a season memorable? Most notably, it is when somehow we have been changed, shaped or perhaps reshaped, and more than likely are better for the experience. That is also often the outcome of our college days, no matter where we have studied. Eager seekers of knowledge come ready to learn, grow and take on the world.

But a university is memorable to more than its students. Its greater family – made up of teachers, administrators, community supporters and residents – are affected by a special place that molds us, influences us, alters us and becomes a genuine and lasting memory. The photos in this book attempt to capture those sights and feelings, to show visually the place the SVSU campus holds in the hearts and minds of all who have experienced it, in a variety of ways. A university is not a typical organization or business. Like life itself, its activities run from the silly to the sublime, from the serious to the sentimental. We engage the life of the mind and enjoy the pleasures of the environment; we embrace the spirit of mental and physical competition both in the classroom and on the playing field. These photos show the range of human activities and events; they celebrate the ages and stages, artists and athletes, learners and teachers, visitors and residents, and those who give as well as those who gratefully receive.

The photos in this book show as well the remarkable contrasts that take place … in this place … because of this place. SVSU is a collection of neighborhoods, from the foundry and racing performance lab to the athletic fields and art gallery. A business center, a student center, a recital hall, a dining hall, a theatre stage or a Cardinal Cage – all parts of the larger whole where the hum of activity, the buzz of conversation, the quick rotation through turnstiles, represent the coming and going of those who will be transformed by this place.

SVSU … This memorable destination is a place through which thousands of alumni have passed and, in so doing, have crossed the threshold from youth to adulthood. This location is a space where countless teachers and professionals, skilled employees and support staff, have spent some of their finest hours while becoming better at what they do or becoming better friends with colleagues. This venue for events and celebrations, for orientation and commencement, for weddings and farewells, is itself tied to the cycle of the year. Like the people who comprise it, a university lives and breathes and, like them, marks the passage of time through the seasons.

The Editors

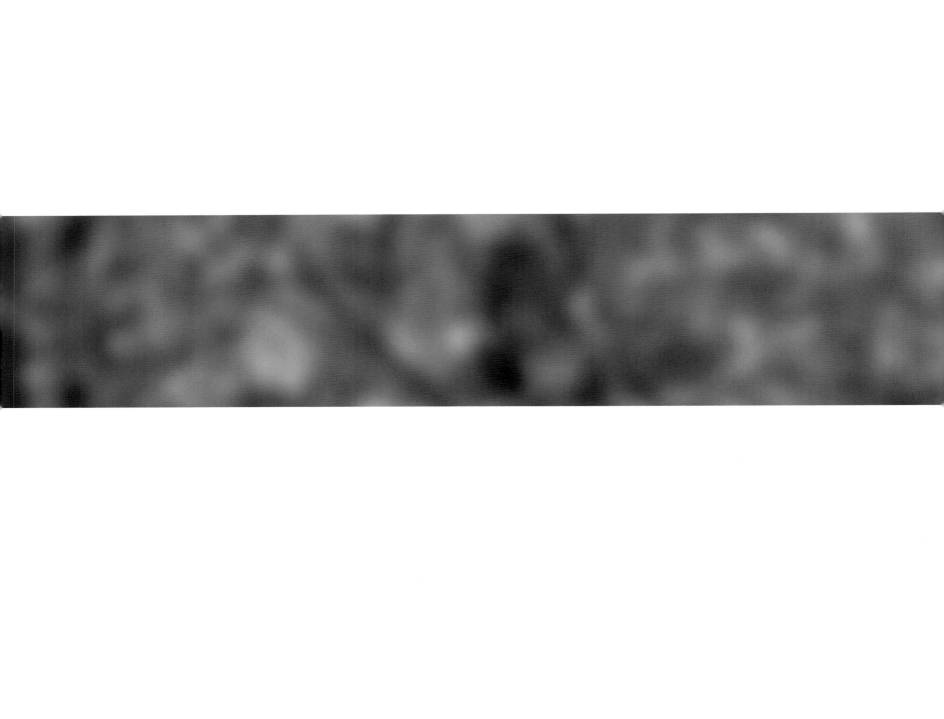

FALL

Now light is less; noon skies are wide and deep.
Theodore Roethke, "Slow Season"

HOME TEAM
PRIDE
LIFTS SPIRITS HIGH.

INSIDE. OUTDOORS.

EVERYWHERE
ARE AUTUMN MOMENTS ON CAMPUS.

27

HELPING
HANDS REACH OUT TO THE REGION.

CRISP DAYS
CRACKLE
WITH ACTIVITY.

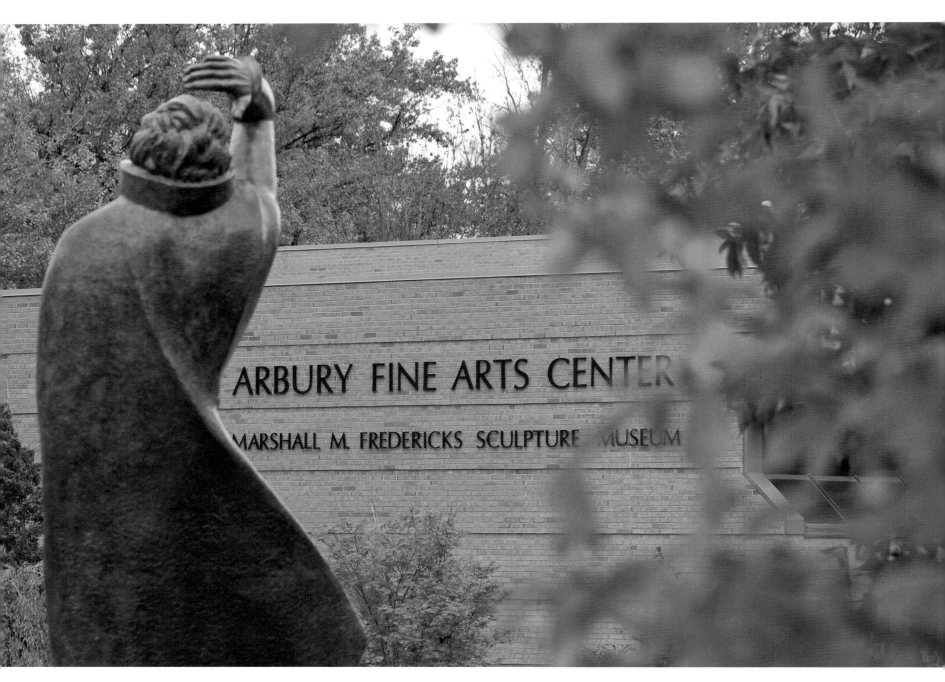

POET BYRON'S
ARTFUL
GUARD.

FLEETING MOMENTS
FRAMED BY A BACKDROP OF AUTUMN'S MAJESTY.

WINTER

It was beginning winter, an in-between time.
Theodore Roethke, "The Lost Son"

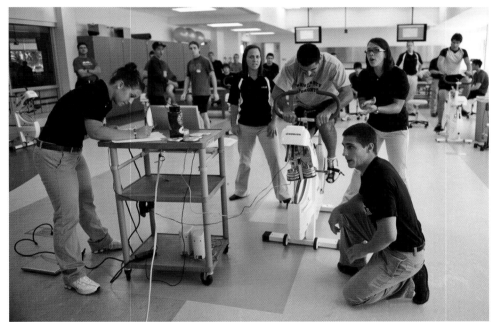

MAGICAL
MOMENTS THAT WARM UP A WINTERY CAMPUS.

71

HUSHED SETTINGS IN A
PRISTINE
LANDSCAPE.

SILLY AND STUDIOUS
ON A WINTER'S DAY.

"If a nation expects to be ignorant and free, in a state o

Student
Technology
Center
2nd Floor

MELVIN J.
ZAHNOW
LIBRARY

Einstein's
Food Court

civilization, it expects what never was and never will be." Thomas Jefferson

93

SHARING.
DARING.
CARING.

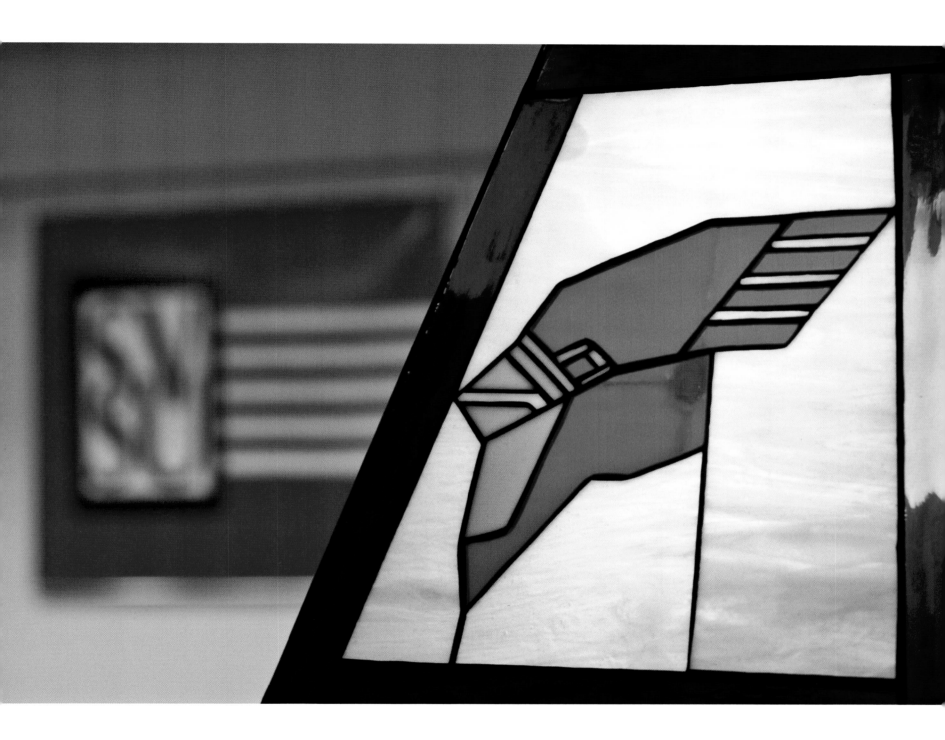

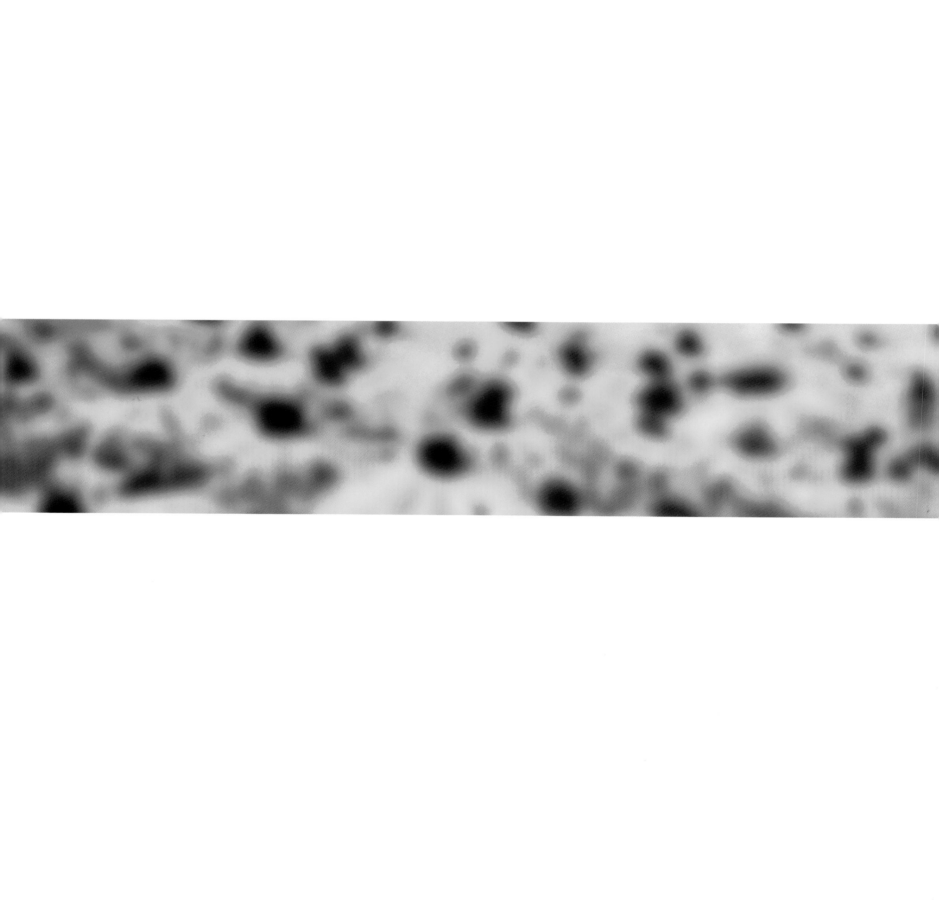

SPRING

I rejoice in the spring, as though no spring ever had been.
Theodore Roethke, "Vernal Sentiment"

BURGEONING BLOSSOMS
ANNOUNCE WINTER'S RETREAT.

CURTISS HALL

Ah,
THE SMELL, THE SIGHTS,
THE SENSE OF SPRING'S ARRIVAL.

113

TIME FOR.
DISCOVERY.

NATURE SIGNALS
HOPE AND PROMISE
FOR THOSE WHO DARE TO DREAM.

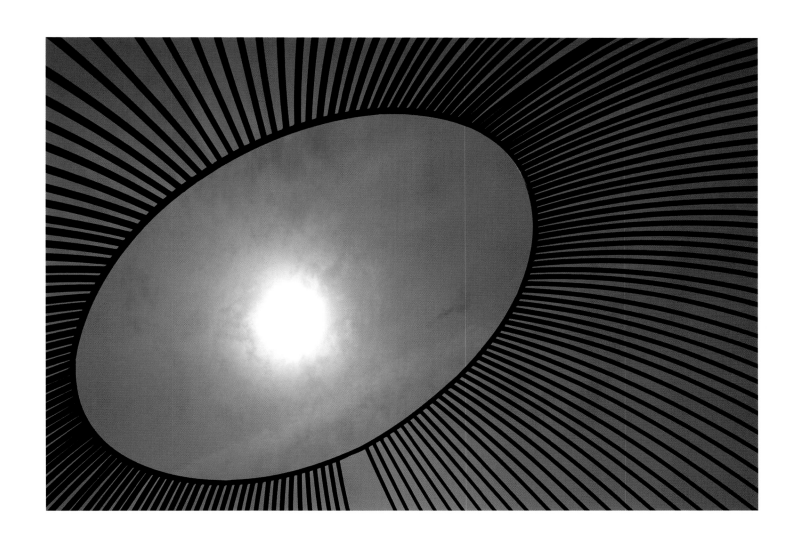

SUMMER

And all the waters of all the streams
Sang in my veins that summer day.

Theodore Roethke, "The Waking"

147

A CAMPUS BRIMS WITH
SUMMER'S
JUBILANT CELEBRATION.

154

WE ARE ALL
PLAYERS
ON THE STAGE OF LIFE.

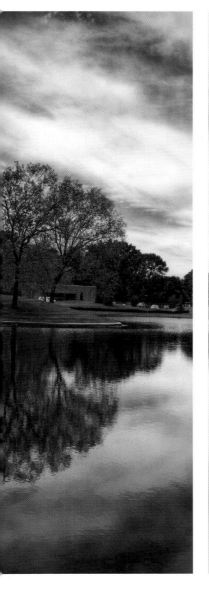

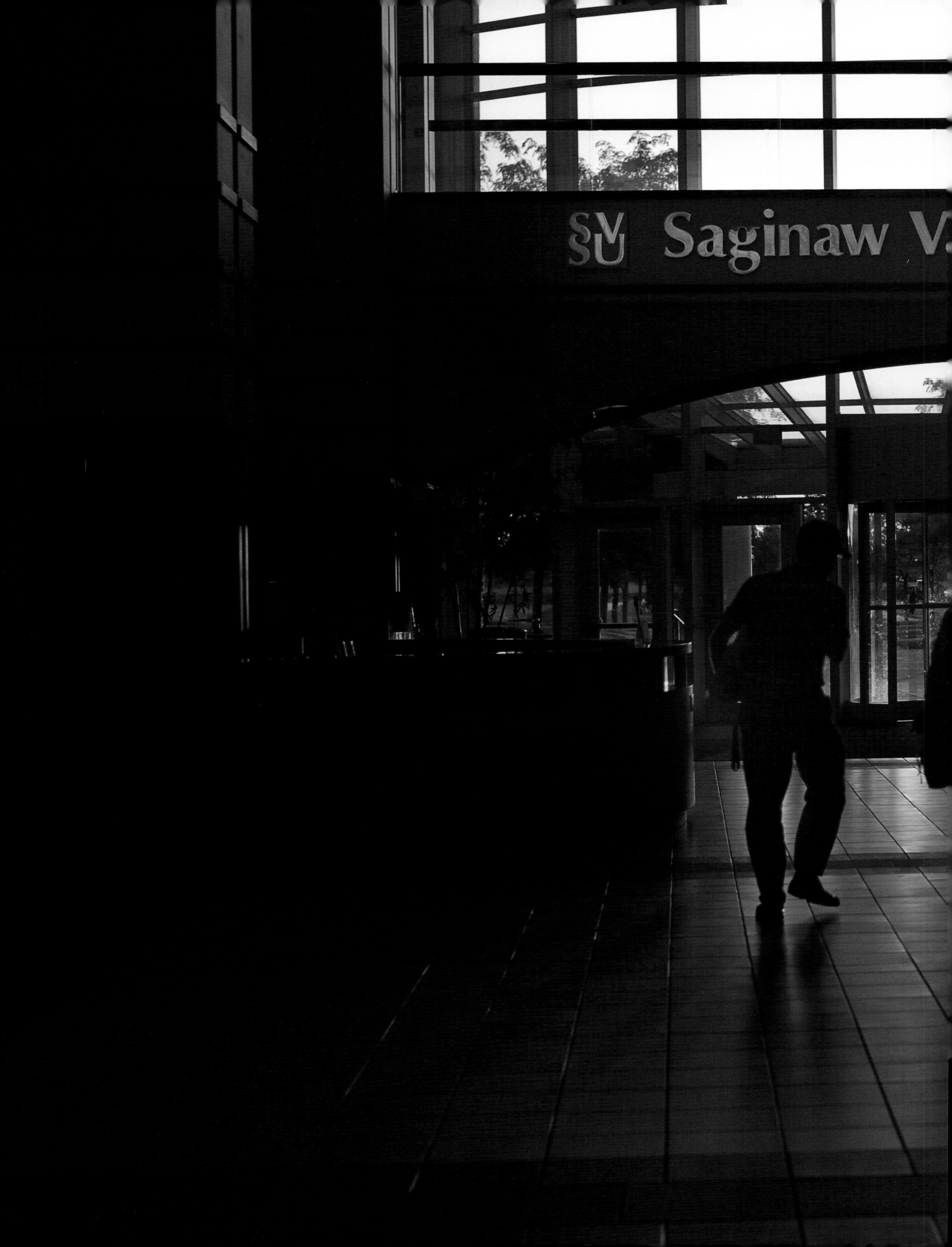
SVSU Saginaw V

Global Community

Pine Grove
Building 7001

THE SEASON FOR SAYING
GOODBYE,
UNTIL AUTUMN'S RETURN.

STATE UNIVERSITY

CHEMISTRY 111
COURSE STRUCTURE

* Basic requirement: H.S. Chemistry or Chem 101

* Syllabus & grading

* Lecture & recitation

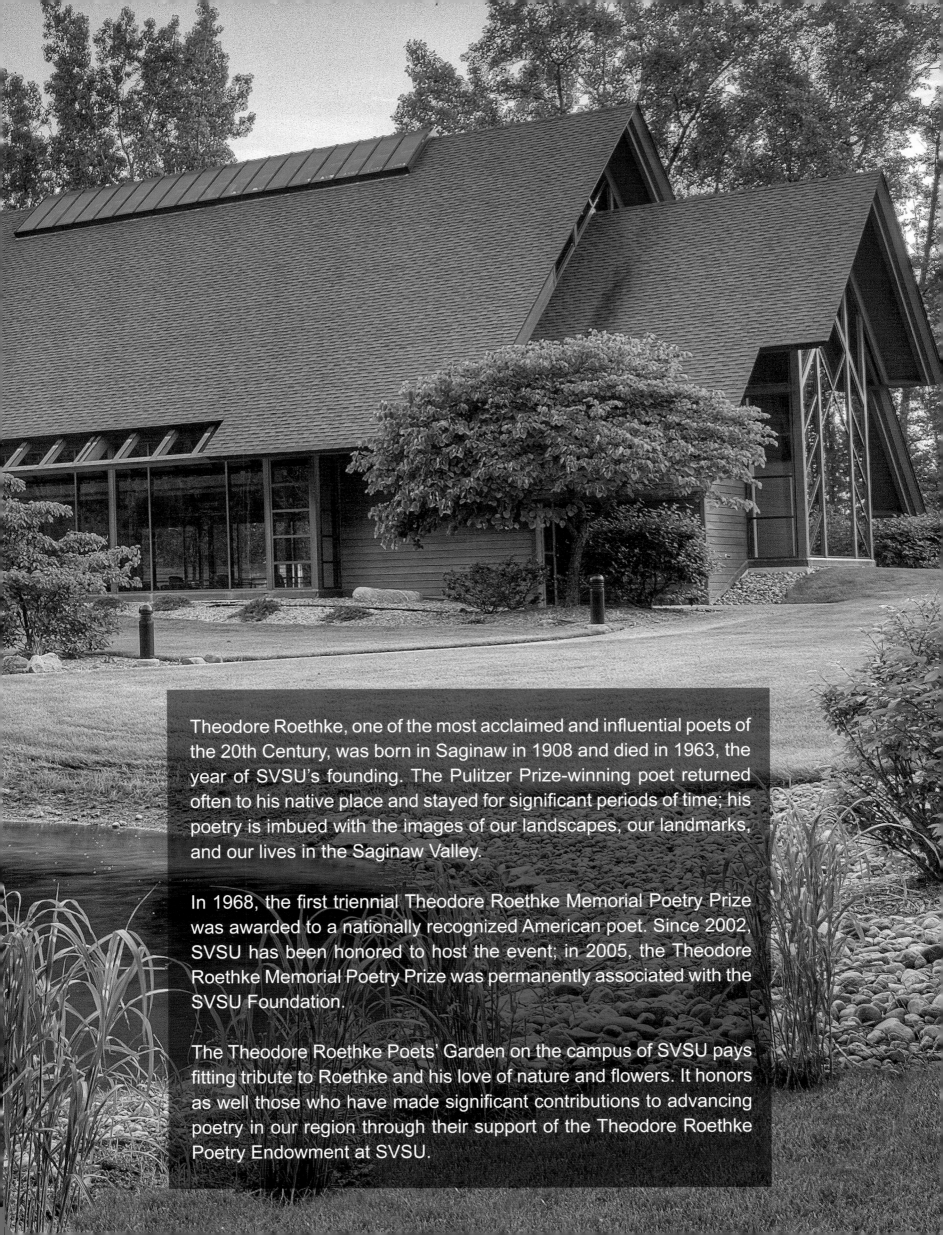

Theodore Roethke, one of the most acclaimed and influential poets of the 20th Century, was born in Saginaw in 1908 and died in 1963, the year of SVSU's founding. The Pulitzer Prize-winning poet returned often to his native place and stayed for significant periods of time; his poetry is imbued with the images of our landscapes, our landmarks, and our lives in the Saginaw Valley.

In 1968, the first triennial Theodore Roethke Memorial Poetry Prize was awarded to a nationally recognized American poet. Since 2002, SVSU has been honored to host the event; in 2005, the Theodore Roethke Memorial Poetry Prize was permanently associated with the SVSU Foundation.

The Theodore Roethke Poets' Garden on the campus of SVSU pays fitting tribute to Roethke and his love of nature and flowers. It honors as well those who have made significant contributions to advancing poetry in our region through their support of the Theodore Roethke Poetry Endowment at SVSU.

Index

Index

Index

Index